Adult addiction to alcohol and other drugs is one of socie. problems. This book is dedicated to the forgotten victims...th Many thanks to the professionals who are dedicated to their work They have inspired, educated and encouraged me to make this book possible.

WOODLAND PRESS
99 WOODLAND CIRCLE
MINNEAPOLIS, MN 55424
(952) 926-2665

PRINTED IN THE U.S.A.

ABOUT THIS BOOK

This book was created to help children understand addiction when someone in their family has a problem. Families with addiction problems to alcohol and other drugs often have difficulties with communication and especially about feelings. They have developed the rules of "don't talk, don't trust and don't feel" to cope with the stresses of addiction.

Children may be reluctant to share thoughts and feelings at first and this right must be respected. Adults may share their own experiences and feelings and ask who might have similar or different feelings. Respect children's need for time and space to work through denial and isolation. They may have realistic fears of punishment. When they are ready to share it is important to give them uninterrupted time and attention.

The art process allows children to express thoughts, feelings and perceptions about themselves and others. Symbolically they learn to recognize and express feelings common to family problems. Conflicts can be resolved and self esteem is increased while coping skills are developed.

Educational concepts are presented in six units to help children understand addictions and how to cope with problems. Reading from additional books is suggested. Each child will need a small box of crayons to illustrate their book. Crayons are suggested because they are more effective than markers for expressing feelings. Older children may prefer colored pencils for more details.

Ask children to draw any picture that comes to mind as they read the words on each page. Do not make suggestions. Trust the child to make decisions about what and when to draw. Encourage ideas and expressions rather than drawing ability. During difficult emotional times, children often regress and scribble, erase, cross-out, draw something unrelated or leave the page blank. This is all right. It is the beginning of finding a voice for thoughts and feelings that are difficult to express.

This book was designed to help children understand basic concepts of drug and alcohol addiction and it's effect on the family and develop healthy coping skills. Drawing encourages verbal communication and reveals children's concerns and misconceptions. The following objectives are included in the text and may be stressed by additional reading from suggested books.

FOR ADULTS:

Any long term illness creates an atmosphere of tension and anxiety. Alcohol and drug addiction is especially problematic because it is a disease seldom understood by others. In most families it is a secret denied inside and outside the home and the impact is minimized.

Denial and the need to maintain it results in negative and destructive problems that no one can deal with because the problem hasn't been identified. Children feel confused seeing problems that no one else seems to see. Problems need to be acknowledged and discussed.

Children need to know about the effects of drug and alcohol addiction so they can develop skills for coping with the problems. Children need to know they did not cause the problem and cannot fix the problem.

It is difficult for children to see a parent as "bad" so they often assume the blame and see themselves as "bad". They need to know that adults, including parents, are not perfect. Mistakes are made and require restitution and apologies. They can be encouraged to develop trust and faith in a higher non-human power.

It is important not to let the problem overshadow children's developmental needs. Young children can become the forgotten victims of a parent's addiction. They need to know they are lovable and special, and allowed to be their natural selves. They can be expected to act their age but not required to act older than they are.

Time and attention from others helps children recognize their personal strengths and be able to love and accept themselves. Families often retreat from others to keep their secret. Children need community involvement so they can see other families model healthy and normal expression of feelings, intimacy, closeness, fun and problem solving.

School activities and clubs can help children gain support and develop social skills. Support groups for children in addicted families can help them learn they are not alone and gain needed skills.

Children worry about what will happen to them and their parents. They struggle with feelings of guilt, sadness, helplessness, fear and anger. They freeze overwhelming feelings and learn to avoid difficult feelings by trying not to care and putting on a false self to please others. It may be difficult to recognize their inner pain.

Children absorb the value and respect parents have for them and this becomes the basis of their own self esteem. They need appropriate discipline and limits so they learn not to abuse or offend others and respect and protect rights to their own thoughts, feelings, behaviors and bodies. They need rules, reasons for those rules, and choices with natural consequences. Age appropriate chores and responsibilities provide structure and areas of control in their lives. They need to learn how to follow healthy rules . . . and how to break unhealthy rules.

Weekly family meetings can be scheduled to discuss problems and solutions. Children can learn the difference between wants and needs. Families also need to plan time to play games and have fun together.

ADDITIONAL READING FOR CHILDREN:

Black, Claudia. MY DAD LOVES ME. MY DAD HAS A DISEASE. Denver, CO. MAC publishing, 1982

Davis, Diane. SOMETHING IS WRONG AT MY HOUSE. Seattle, WA. Parenting Press, 1985

DiGiovanni, Kathe. MY HOUSE IS DIFFERENT. Minneapolis, MN Hazelden, 1989

Hall, Lindsey & Cohn, Leigh. DEAR KIDS OF ALCOHOLICS. Carlsbad, CA. Gurz Books, 1988

O'Connor, Diane. I CAN BE ME. Deerfield Beach, FL. Health Communications, 1987

Rosenberg, Maxine. NOT MY FAMILY. N.Y., N.Y. Bradbury Press, 1988

Sanford, Doris. I KNOW THE WORLD'S WORST SECRET. Portland, OR. Multnomah Press, 1987

Seixas, Judisth. LIVING WITH A PARENT WHO TAKES DRUGS. S. Greenwillow Books, 1989

Sinberg, Janet & Daley, Dennis. I CAN TALK ABOUT WHAT HURTS. Minneapolis, MN. Hazelden, 1989

Taylor, Clark. THE HOUSE THAT CRACK BUILT. San Francisco, CA. Chronicle Books, 1992

Vigna, Judith. I WISH DADDY DIDN'T DRINK SO MUCH. Morton Grove, IL. Albert Whitman & Co., 1988

ADDITIONAL READING FOR PARENTS:

Clarke, Gesme, London & Brundage, HELP! For kids and parents about drugs. San Francisco, CA. Harper, 1993

ADDITIONAL READING FOR PARENTS WHO GREW UP IN AN ADDICTED FAMILY:

Beattie, Melody. BEYOND CO DEPENDENCY. N.Y., N.Y. Harper/Hazelden, 1989

Mellody, Pia. FACING CoDEPENDENCY. N.Y., N.Y. Harper & Row, 1989

Woititz, Janet. LIFE SKILLS FOR ADULT CHILDREN. Deerfield Beach, FL. Health Communications, 1991

FOR ADULTS LEADING CHILDREN'S SUPPORT GROUPS:

Hastings, Jill & Typo, Marion. AN ELEPHANT IN THE LIVING ROOM. Children's Book and Leader's guide.

Muldoon, Joseph. MY TURN: A SUPPORT GROUP FOR CHILDREN AFFECTED BY ALCOHOLISM. Book & guide.

ADDITIONAL RESOURCES:

ALANON FAMILY GROUP HEADQUARTERS
PO Box 868
Midtown Station, New York, NY 10018
800-344-2666

CHILDREN OF ALCOHOLICS FOUNDATION, INC.
PO Box 4815
New York, NY 10163
800-359-COAF

DEACONESS PRESS BOOKS (Catalogue)
PROMOTING HEALTHY LIVING
  FOR KIDS AND ADULTS
2450 Riverside Ave. South
Minneapolis, MN 55454
1-800-544-8207   (612) 672-4180

FEELINGS GAMES & AFFIRMATIONS (Catalogue)
Carol Gesme
4036 Kerry Court
Minnetonka MN 55345
(612) 938-9163

COMMUNITY INTERVENTION (Catalogue)
529 S 7th St. Suite 570
Minneapolis, MN 55425
800-328-0417

HAZELDEN EDUCATIONAL MATERIALS (Catalogue)
15251 Pleasant Valley Rd
PO Box 176
Center City, MN 55012-0176
1-800-328-9000

FOR CHILDREN:

ALL FAMILIES HAVE PROBLEMS. PROBLEMS CAUSED BY DRUGS OR ALCOHOL ARE OFTEN HARDER TO TALK ABOUT. THIS BOOK WILL TEACH YOU SOME FACTS TO HELP YOU BEGIN TO UNDERSTAND THE PROBLEMS AND HOW TO TAKE BETTER CARE OF YOURSELF.

THIS IS YOUR BOOK YOU WILL MAKE IT SPECIAL AS YOU DRAW THE PICTURES THAT COME INTO YOUR MIND AS YOU READ THE WORDS ON EACH PAGE. MOST CHILDREN FIND IT IS EASIER TO DRAW PICTURES ABOUT SOME THINGS THAN IT IS TO TALK ABOUT THEM. YOU DO NOT HAVE TO BE ABLE TO DRAW WELL TO ADD YOUR THOUGHTS AND FEELINGS TO THIS BOOK. YOU WILL NEED JUST A SMALL BOX OF CRAYONS TO DRAW LINES AND SHAPES AND MAYBE A FEW WORDS TO TELL WHAT YOU THINK OR FEEL. THERE IS NO RIGHT OR WRONG WAY. YOU CAN DO IT YOUR WAY.

BEGIN WITH THE FIRST PAGE AND DO THE PAGES IN ORDER. DON'T SKIP PAGES. WHEN YOU HAVE FINISHED A FEW PAGES SHARE YOUR WORK WITH AN ADULT WHO CARES ABOUT YOU AND WITH WHOM YOU FEEL COMFORTABLE TALKING. MOST CHILDREN FEEL BETTER AFTER THEY HAVE TALKED ABOUT THEIR FEELINGS WITH SOMEONE. YOU MAY LEARN THAT PEOPLE ARE ALREADY AWARE OF WHAT YOU THOUGHT WAS YOUR SECRET PROBLEM. YOU ARE NOT ALONE. ALMOST EVERY FAMILY HAS SOMEONE THEY LOVE WITH A PROBLEM WITH ALCOHOL OR OTHER DRUGS.

IT IS IMPORTANT TO LEARN HOW TO SHARE HONEST THOUGHTS AND FEELINGS. IT IS THE FIRST STEP FOR MAKING CHANGES.

A <u>HABIT</u> is something people have done so often they do it without thinking much about it. Some habits are <u>good</u> for you like and ... (draw some more)

Draw a ☆ by the good habits you have!

Other habits are called <u>BAD HABITS</u> because they are not good for people like...

too much

CANDY

Junk food

BAD words

BEER

(Draw an ✓ on those you have and draw some more)

Next... draw a circle around any you <u>tried</u> to but <u>couldn't</u> change.

2. Bad habits can be <u>very</u> hard to change... but can be!

Bad habits can become very difficult <u>problems</u>! My family has a problem that is hard to talk about ...
(draw the problem)

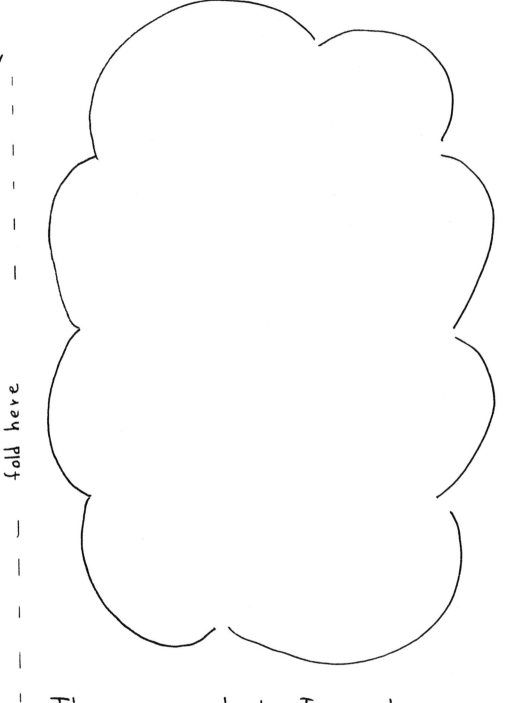

This is what I wish could happen. (draw and fold) 3.

fold here

This is a picture of the person with a problem...

There are things I like about this person. (draw some)

It is O.K. to love the person and hate the problem.

4.

This is _me_ doing things I _like_ to do...

I am an _important_ person in my family!

Using drugs or alcohol can become a bad habit. Addiction means people have trouble stopping even when they know it is harming them or others. It is a serious disease. Children may try different ways to stop the person from drinking or using drugs.

6. Children can't <u>cause</u> or <u>stop</u> addiction.

Facts About Alcohol And Other Drugs

Some <u>drugs</u> bought in a drugstore can help heal people if they are used with care. Too much can be harmful and is called <u>drug abuse.</u>

<u>Nicotine</u> is a drug found in cigarettes and can cause cancer, heart and lung disease.

<u>Alcohol</u> is a drug found in drinks like beer, wine gin, vodka, scotch and whiskey. It can affect people's health and behavior badly. When people can't control the amount they drink, they have a disease called <u>alcoholism.</u>

Other drugs are <u>illegal</u> and are a problem for those who use them and the people around them. Cocaine, crack, LSD and marijuana can harm the brain and change the way people think and feel.

People can get <u>high</u> or <u>drunk</u> and act mean or weird from too much drugs or alcohol.

Addicted people can go to a <u>treatment center</u> to get help. There are also <u>support groups</u> for adults, teens and children.

7.

Drugs and alcohol can make "good" people <u>act</u> "bad." Sometimes people who are addicted have <u>a</u> hard time showing their care or love. They may not be fun to live with! (draw the way people change.)

<u>Before</u> using   <u>After</u> using

8. Addicted people sometimes act in hurtful ways. It can be scary and embarrassing.

Families with addiction problems may make <u>unfair</u> rules to make things seem O.K. like:

Don't tell the family secret.
Don't trust other people.
Don't feel difficult feelings.

These rules can be confusing and unhealthy.
(✶ the rules you think are O.K.)
(✓ the rules you would like to change.)

Write some <u>new rules</u> you would like to make.

_____

_____

_____

_____

This book can help you and your family make some changes. 9.

People in families where there is addiction have <u>many</u> <u>feelings</u> but they <u>don't</u> <u>talk</u> <u>about</u> <u>them</u>. Many people drink or take drugs to <u>not</u> feel or think about unpleasant things.

But...

10. This brings <u>more</u> problems and difficult feelings.

Addiction brings <u>change</u>. There will be many feelings.

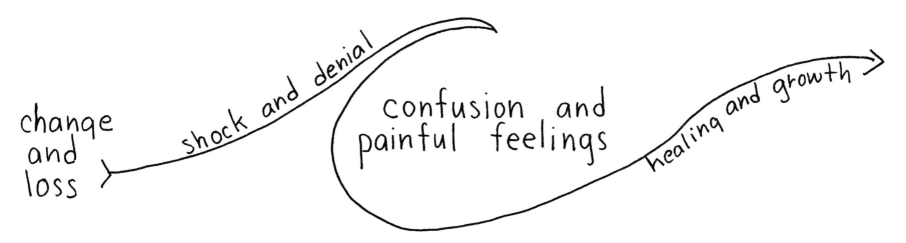

Change brings <u>loss</u> and <u>gains</u>.

The pain from loss is called <u>GRIEF</u>.

Grief comes and goes like ocean <u>waves</u>.

What have <u>you</u> lost?

Feelings are something people feel in their body.

Close your eyes and
think about a time
you felt a feeling and
decide where you feel
that feeling in your
body.

Color that place
with a color.

sad - blue
afraid - black
guilty - brown
angry - red
jealous - green
nervous - orange
happy - yellow

People often stuff feelings <u>inside</u> that are too scary or hurt too much to feel. This wastes energy and can make people feel <u>sick</u> or <u>tired</u>. It can cause aches and pains.

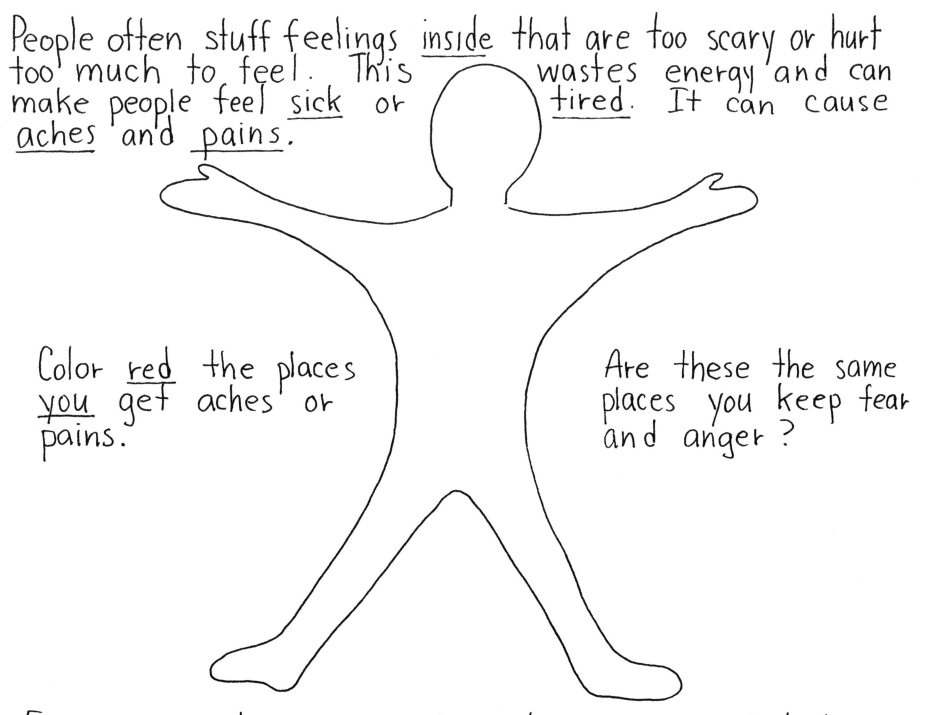

Color <u>red</u> the places <u>you</u> get aches or pains.

Are these the same places you keep fear and anger?

Exercise, sports, music, art, writing, play, and talking are all good ways to let feelings out!

13.

Sometimes people put on a mask to cover feelings of being scared, lonely, worried, sad, mad or even happy. They want to pretend nothing is wrong and they want people to like them. (draw feeling faces and write the word for feelings you sometimes try to hide.)

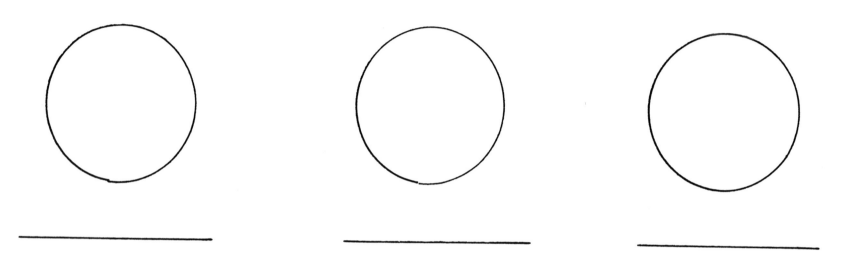

_____   _____   _____

Draw below ↓ and write the name for the "pretend" feeling mask you use.

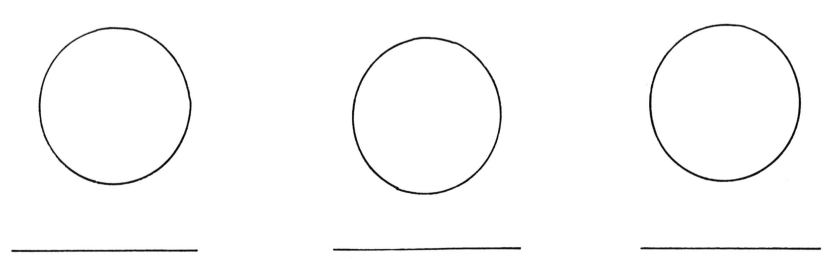

14.

_____   _____   _____

People can't share all feelings _all_ the time. Sometimes _defenses_ are needed to protect people... but they can be like walls between them and others and they can make people feel very lonely. Are there ways you protect yourself but end up feeling lonely?

People feel closer to others when they can share feelings instead of hiding them.

Check the feelings you feel sometimes (v) or if often (vvv). Underline the words you don't know.

scared	nervous	important
brave	sad	empty
lonely	unloved	disgusted
confused	ignored	jealous
proud	angry	shamed
loved	afraid	embarrassed
cheated	excited	frustrated
miserable	bored	disappointed
furious	special	guilty
hurt	happy	worried

16.

Feelings are all O.K. !!!

Anger can give you power to take care of yourself.

Guilt can help you change your behavior.

Pain can help you grow stronger.

Fear can help you protect yourself.

People can learn more about feelings.

Anger kept inside too long becomes rage.

Fear kept inside too long becomes panic.

Pain kept inside too long becomes helplessness.

Guilt kept inside too long becomes shame.

Feelings affect the things you do or say. You are responsible for the behavior you choose!

17.

I feel _frightened_ when... (draw something that scares you.)

18. Drawing something scary can make it less powerful!

I feel <u>angry</u> when   and I ... (draw what you do)
(draw what gets you angry)

Parents feel <u>angry</u> when   and they... (draw what they do)

Sometimes people that are addicted let anger out in ways that <u>hurt others.</u> It is important to learn to let anger out in ways that <u>will not</u> hurt people or things. O.K. ways are:
(★ your favorite ways)

1. Saying "I am angry because..."

2. Count to 10 "inside" and then decide what to do.

3. Writing in a journal.

4. Walking fast.

5. Writing an angry letter and tearing it into small pieces instead of mailing it.

6. Scribbling hard on an old newspaper with a red crayon and scrunch it into a ball to toss at a wall.

7. Stomping your feet or punching a pillow.

8. Yelling into a pillow or in the shower.

20. Let anger out early before it grows and <u>explodes.</u>

Sometimes I feel _sad_... (draw something you feel sad about or a time you felt very sad.)

Crying is O.K. It lets the sadness out.

Children may feel _different_ or _lonely_ if they can't bring friends home or if people at home are busy.

Support groups can help children learn to ask for what they need. Even when they can't get what they need from their family they may feel better talking to others with similar problems.

22.

Sometimes I feel helpless... (draw something you <u>tried</u> to change
about the problem)

Children can't cause or <u>fix</u> adult problems of addiction.
They <u>can't</u> <u>control</u> other people's feelings either.   23.

It's O.K. to have problems. Everyone has problems. (draw some problems you have)

Children can solve <u>some</u> problems themselves. (circle those) Children can't solve some problems but they can be shared with other caring people. (draw X on the problems <u>you</u> can't solve.)

24.

Problems <u>can be solved</u> in healthy ways. (* the things you do)

Choose a good time to talk about the problem.

Decide if the problem is yours. If so...
    say "I have a problem when you... (be specific)
    and I feel...
    and I would like you to..."
    Listen to what they say.

Be responsible for your own behavior.

Think about yours and others needs.

Learn to make good choices.

Avoid power struggles. Don't hit, yell or name call.

Say "I'm sorry" when you really are.

Ask for help when really needed.

Remember... you can't change others... only yourself.

Children feel scared or angry when <u>parents</u> <u>fight</u>....

26. Children don't need to get involved. They can <u>leave</u> the room and turn on TV, or a radio so they can't hear. It's the parents problem...not the children's !!!

When someone has an addiction <u>everyone</u> in the family is affected. The family gets out of balance because so much attention goes to the problem. Children may try different ways to get the attention they need or to make things O.K. These ways can become bad habits.

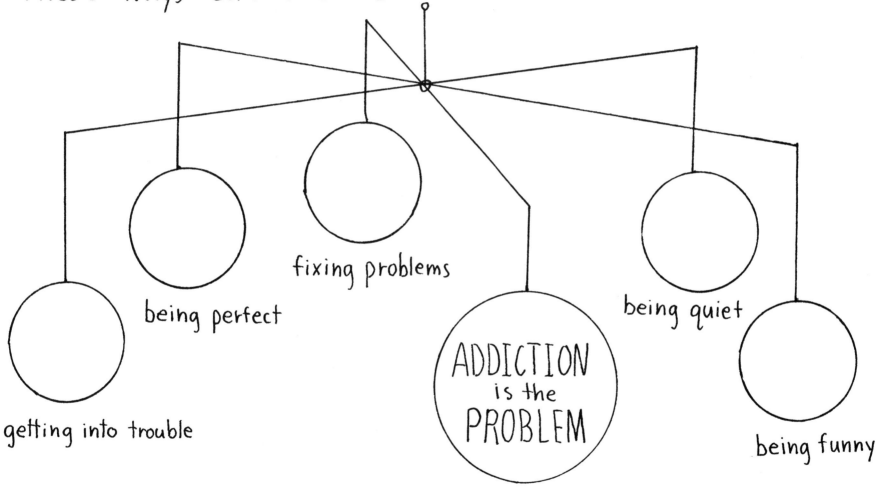

fixing problems

being perfect

being quiet

getting into trouble

ADDICTION
is the
PROBLEM

being funny

Children <u>can't</u> change the addicted person and the family. <u>They</u> can only change <u>themselves</u>.

When children are <u>often</u>... (draw x by the things <u>you</u> do and ⭐ what <u>you can learn</u>.)

<u>Being perfect</u> at home or school thinking all the problems will end if they never cause any problems...
   <u>They can learn</u> no one is perfect and it is O.K. to make mistakes. Children need to have fun!

<u>Getting into trouble</u> by blaming others, acting angry and even causing problems to get attention...
   <u>They can learn</u> how to get along better with others and to express anger in O.K. ways. They can try harder in school and get attention in good ways.

<u>Being funny</u> and making jokes and always acting very happy to hide sadness or cheer up others...
   <u>They can learn</u> it is O.K. to be serious, smart and helpful. They don't always have to be funny. They can share their sad and angry feelings too.

<u>Being quiet</u> or staying away to avoid problems or disturbing others...
   <u>They can learn</u> they are important too and need to learn how to say what they think and feel

28.

Making decisions is important!

1. Name the problem _____

2. List: Choices | good and bad—→ Consequences | Feelings

_____	_____	_____
_____	_____	_____
_____	_____	_____
_____	_____	_____

3. Make your decison _____

_____

Parents, relatives, teachers, friends, TV, movies, books, and others effect choices. Make your own decisions. Don't be afraid to say "no" to something that isn't good for you or could hurt you.

It isn't <u>safe</u> to ride in a car with someone drunk or high on drugs... or with someone acting crazy because they can't get them. It is <u>not</u> a good time to share feelings.

Every child needs to know who they can call for help or a ride home. They need phone numbers and money.
People I can call:

name _____   phone number _____

_____   _____

Everyone needs a place they can feel <u>safe</u>. (draw a real or pretend place where you feel safe. Add someone or something to protect you if you want that.)

Children can ask for help.

Children _need_ love, attention, healthy food, shelter and protection.

Children need someone to _help them_ when they are sick or feel frightened, lonely or sad... or when they need protection or have problems with school work... or just want to have fun.

They need family and friends who _care_ about them and like to be with them. Friends can be older or younger. Some you can trust to talk with about your life. Some you can just be with to have _fun!_

Pets can be good friends. They can be very good _listeners!_

Groups in school or other places can be for fun, learning and support. School counselors can help.

Everyone needs help from others sometimes.

Many people __care__ about you and your family.
(write their name and put the number in the circle)

1. _____

2. _____

3. _____

4. _____

5. _____

6. _____

7. _____

8. _____

9. _____

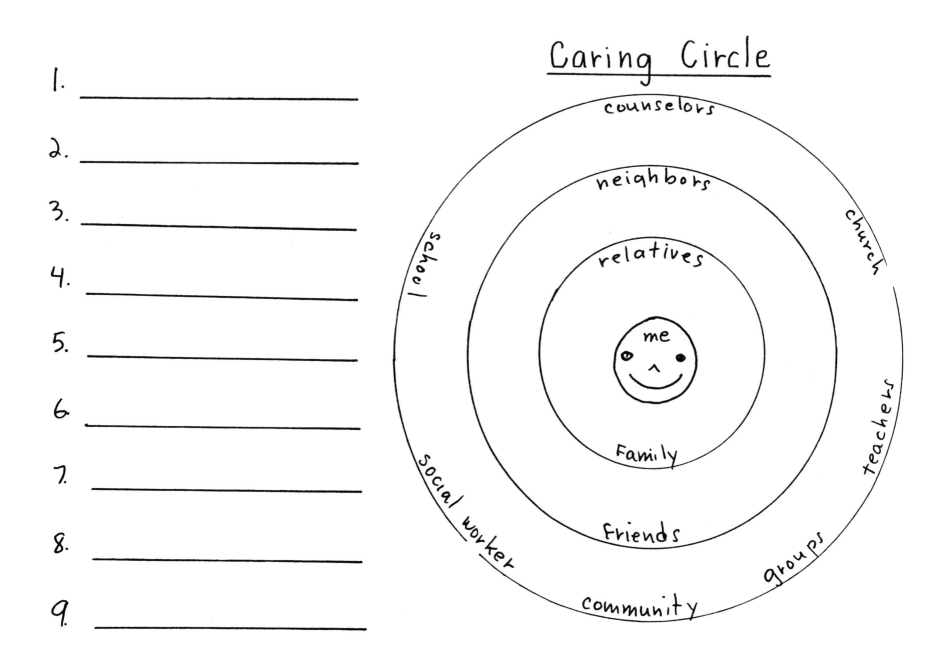

Caring Circle

counselors

neighbors

church

school

relatives

me

teachers

social worker

Family

friends

groups

community

Children can do good things for themselves:

(draw a ☆ on the ___ if you do those things now.)
(draw a ✓ on the ___ if you will try to begin doing those things)

___ Feel all feelings. Share some with friends

___ Stop trying to fix other people's problems.

___ Know they are not to blame for their parent's problems.

___ Say "no" to things that aren't good for them.

___ Practice making good decisions.

___ Say something good to others and themselves each day.

___ Join a group for fun and learning.

___ Find times to just be themselves and have fun.

___ _____
(add something you think is important!)

34. ___ _____

Everyone has something they do well... or feel proud about.

(draw what others say you do well)

(draw something you like about yourself)

People need to like themselves before others can like them !

Someone in my family has a problem with alcohol and other drugs but I can <u>hope</u> for their <u>recovery</u> and something good for us!

36. I will have <u>fun</u> and <u>happy</u> times.

The Drawing Out Feelings Series

This new series designed by Marge Heegaard provides parents and professionals with an organized approach to helping children ages 6-12 cope with feelings resulting from family loss and change.

Designed to be used in an adult/child setting, these workbooks provide age-appropriate educational concepts and questions to help children identify and accept their feelings. Children are given the opportunity to work out their emotions during difficult times while learning to recognize acceptable behavior, and conflicts can be resolved and self-esteem increased while the coping skills for loss and change are being developed.

All four titles are formatted so that children can easily illustrate their answers to the important questions in the text.

When Something Terrible Happens

A workbook to help children deal with their feelings about traumatic events.

Empowers children to explore feelings, and reduces nightmares and post-traumatic stress symptoms. "This healing book...combines story, pictures, information, and art therapy in a way that appeals to children." —Stephanie Frogge, Director of Victim Outreach, M.A.D.D.

Ages 6-12, 36 pp, 11 x 8 1/2"
trade paperback, ISBN 0-9620502-3-7

When Mom and Dad Separate

A workbook to help children deal with their feelings about separation/divorce

This bestselling workbook helps youngsters discuss the basic concepts of marriage and divorce, allowing them to work through all the powerful and confusing feelings resulting from their parents' decision to separate.

Ages 6-12, 36 pp, 11 x 8 1/2"
trade paperback, ISBN 0-9620502-2-9

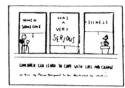

When Someone Has a Very Serious Illness

A workbook to help children deal with their feelings about serious illness.

An excellent resource for helping children learn the basic concepts of illness and various age-appropriate ways of coping with someone else's illness. "...offers children a positive tool for coping with those many changes." —Christine Ternand, M.D., Pediatrician

Ages 6-12, 41 pp, 11 x 8 1/2"
trade paperback, ISBN 0-9620502-4-5

When Someone Very Special Dies
Children Can Learn to Cope with Grief

A workbook to help children deal with their feelings about death.

Here is a practical format for allowing children to understand the concept of death and develop coping skills for life. Children, with adult supervision, are invited to illustrate and personalize their loss through art. This workbook encourages the child to identify support systems and personal strengths. "I especially appreciate the design of this book...the child becomes an active participant in pictorially and verbally doing something about [their loss]." —Dean J. Hempel, M.D., Child Psychiatrist

Ages 6-12
36 pp, 11 x 8 1/2"
trade paperback
ISBN 0-9620502-0-2

When a Family Is In Trouble
Children Can Cope With Grief From Drug and Alcohol Addictions

A workbook to help children through the trauma of a parent's chemical dependency problem.

This helpful workbook provides basic information about addictions and encourages healthy coping skills. Children express personal trauma and feelings more easily in pictures than in words, and the pages of this title are perfect to "draw out" those feelings and hurts. There is plenty of room for a child's artwork.

Ages 6-12
36 pp, 11 x 8 1/2"
trade paperback
ISBN 0-9620502-7-X

When a Parent Marries Again

A workbook to help children deal with their feelings about stepfamilies.

This book helps kids sort through unrealistic expectations, different values, divided loyalties, and family histories. It helps reduce the fear and stress surrounding remarriage and promotes greater family unity.

Ages 6-12, 36 pp, 11 x 8 1/2"
trade paperback, ISBN 0-9620502-6-1

Facilitator Guide For **DRAWING OUT FEELINGS**

for
When Someone Very Special Dies
When Something Terrible Happens
When Someone Has a Very Serious Illness
When Mom and Dad Separate

Structure and suggestions for helping children, individually or in groups, cope with feelings from family change. Includes directions for six organized sessions for each of the four workbooks.
99 pp. 8½x11 ISBN 0-9620502-5-3

SEND THIS INFORMATION TO ORDER

For Adults

Grief - A Natural Reaction to Loss

$9.95 PBK

6 x 9 • 92 PAGES